WALKING THROUGH THE WILDERNESS

A 60 DAY DEVOTIONAL

VORONICA WILLIAMS

Walking through the wilderness

Copyright © 2018

by Voronica Williams

All rights reserved

Printed in the United States of America. This document is geared towards providing exact and reliable information in regards to the topic and issues covered. The publication is sold on the idea that the publisher is not required to render accounting, officially permitted, or otherwise, qualified services. If advice is necessary, legal or professional, a practiced individual in the profession should be ordered.

From a Declaration of Principles which was accepted and approved equally by a Committee of the American Bar Association and a Committee of Publishers and Associations.

In no way is it legal to reproduce, duplicate, or transmit any part of this document by either electronic means or in printed format. Recording of this publication is strictly prohibited and any storage of this document is not. allowed unless with written permission from the publisher.

All rights reserved.

ISBN: 978-0-9890673-9-3

Published by:
Sunday Publishing Company
2890 GA 212, Suite 153
Conyers, Georgia
(786) 565-8199
www.sundaypublishingcompany.com

Dedications

I dedicate this devotional to my friends and family that stood by me during one of the toughest times in my life. I give all the praise, honor and glory to God for reminding me of who I was; even when what I had was lost.

Introduction

We all go through difficulties, trials, tribulations, hardships, pain, sorrow, failures and so much more. God doesn't cause everything, yet He allows it all. He is aware of the circumstances, so it is not a surprise or shock to Him. You can either focus on the problem or the promise. You are not at a standstill, He is always leading you through. It may get hard at times, yet His Word is the lamp to your feet and the light to your path. You may cry, fuss, complain, get angry, even feel as if you are not hearing from God; but do not give up. He is right there with you even as you are reading this book. It is you and Him. Reading this may bring back memories and may even hurt just to think about all you have been through over your life. But, God's blessing is always in the midst of the pain. He is leading you with a cloud by day and fire by night. So there is nowhere you can go, that God isn't there. He is Omnipresent (meaning everywhere); He knows exactly how you feel even right now because He is

Omniscient (meaning all-knowing). And He has all the power in the world to change everything because He is Omnipotent (meaning all-power). Keep your eyes on Jesus and watch how your life will start to change. Let God direct your every step and speak to your heart and spirit as you delve into this devotional. So, as you are reading and meditating on what the words are saying to you, write down exactly what God is speaking to your spirit.

"Remember how the Lord your God led you all the way in the wilderness these forty years, to humble and test you in order to know what was in your heart, whether or not you would keep his commands." Deuteronomy 8:2

Trust God even when you cannot see the road ahead!

Day 1: Trust

Trust is something we all should have learned from our parents as a child. We come into the world, and none of us knew anything about trust until we got older. But God tells us in His Word, to place all of our trust in Him. It is such an easy thing for us to say, and yet hard to live out. This is because we try to fix outside things and problems ourselves; instead of allowing God to work in us. Why do we cause more worry, stress and heartache on ourselves, when God is honing, cutting away, stripping and rebuilding what is inside? Sometimes it is the voices that do not really matter, that is the loudest. When you sit and meditate on God's Word, you will hear His still, small voice, and you will discern His vision and purpose for your life. Sometimes, it is also your own thought that frightens you the most. And God doesn't give us a spirit of fear. He wants us to walk in faith and trust that when and if we take a step, then He will open a new door. When we focus on Him, He will give us peace for our worries.

What are you having a hard time letting go of and trusting God in? Is your trust in people or God? If your complete trust is in God, He will lead you to the people that need to cross your path in this season.

"Trust in the Lord with all of your heart and lean not on your own understand." Proverbs 3:5

Day 2: My Plans vs God's Plan

As a child, we all had plans to decide what we wanted to be when we grew up. So many choices from doctors, lawyers, nurses, policemen, scientist or even a soldier. We turn 17 or 18, graduate high school, go to college, and we are now "ready to start life." We find spouses and have children, just to be divorced in less than 2 years. We search and search for happiness, through opportunities with great pay, benefits, security, and a great home in an amazing location. It all looks good on the outside. Things start to fail; we are angry all of the time, complaining over small issues, working too many hours, family falling apart, no passion for the job any longer and now you are becoming weary. Yet, we forgot the most important question. A question most of us were not taught as children. "God, what is Your plan for my life?" Many of us chose our path because either our parents or someone very close to us decided it for us in advance. We end up getting that job or joining the military just to realize that it was not really a part of our plan or God's plan. It was all for comfort. God will allow our comfort zone to be shaken so that we will come to Him and discern our next direction. He is always there to direct you and lead you into your destiny. Every person that exists has a purpose. It's a simple question to ask. Take the worries off of you and give it to Him. Experience the peace of God.

"For I know the plans I have for you," says the Lord. "They are plans for good and not for disaster, to give you a future and a hope." Jeremiah 29:11

Day 3: Sit back and weather the storm

When trouble strikes, we sometimes forget our knowledge of God. We struggle to recall past answers to prayers, specific guidance of the Holy Spirit, and lessons learned in previous crisis. Only the present seems real. Our troubles inhibit clear thinking. In our own strength, we lack sufficient resource and ability to meet life challenges. Yet, God is our only Source. He alone provides what we need. He orchestrates our circumstance for His glory and our benefit. No one enjoys suffering. But in the hand of the Almighty God, trials become tools. No one can see in a storm. It may appear right now that all that you are facing or all the circumstances you are going through is never-ending. In the Bible, when Peter had his eyes on Jesus, he did not allow anything to deter him. He was determined to trust Jesus and walk toward Him on the water. But once he realized there was a storm, trials, persecutions and so much more, he took his eyes off of Jesus. He then started to sink. Jesus was still there with His hand stretched out towards Peter. Well, that is just how our Heavenly Father feels towards His children. Yes, there will be storms, but as long as you keep your eyes on Jesus Christ, you will never fail. Be a passenger and allow God to drive.

"But when he saw the wind, he was afraid and, beginning to sink, cried out, "Lord, save me! Immediately Jesus reached out his hand and caught him." Matthew 14:30-31

Day 4:
Detours on the way to your destiny

Joseph's story is an amazing example of God's setup for a blessing. You may hit a roadblock in your life. Some of them we cause ourselves, some forced by others, the majority of them are put on us by the enemy, and all of them are allowed by God. God will sometimes position roadblocks in front of you that will cause for an immediate decision to stop or go in another direction. I believe God orders our steps along with our stops. Some of the paths God will clearly mark out for you to follow, and others you will have to choose which direction according to the Holy Spirit. No matter which one it is, every roadblock is put up for our protection. It is a detour in the way to get you to your destiny. A lot of times, we fight it, by trying very hard to get through that door that God keeps blocking. By continually hanging out with the friends that are not wise, or trying to force someone to marry you when God is saying "I already have your spouse for you." Sometimes, we block our own purpose by being impatient and not waiting on God. But I believe our Heavenly Father is so merciful and full of grace, that He still prepares our heart desires for our good and His glory. We just have to be patient. The length of time depends on you. Detours are painful; yet necessary. Take the vertical path and remember what God has promised each and every one of us. He is with you always. He will never leave you.

"And we know that God causes everything to work together for the good of those who love God and are called according to his purpose for them." Romans 8:28

Day 5: Obedience leads to Peace

If you feel overwhelmed or confused about a decision that you are trying to make, you are probably caught up in your thoughts and not God's voice. The Bible says, "God is not a God of confusion or disorder, but of peace." He is not the author of confusion. So if you are feeling confused, it is not God's voice speaking in your life right now. If you feel like God told you to do something but you have increasing anxiety because of it, then the wires are probably crossed up. The Bible tells us "Do not worry or be anxious about anything; instead pray about everything. Tell God what you need, and thank Him in advance for all that He has done. Only then you will experience God's peace, which exceeds anything we can understand. His peace will guard your hearts and minds as you live in Christ Jesus." Today, what are you having a difficult time with? Don't take that same problem of today into your tomorrow. Whatever it is, receive peace about it now. It only weighs you down the longer you carry it.

"For God is not a God of disorder but of peace as in all the congregations of the Lord's people." 1 Corinthians 14:33

Day 6: Steps of Faith

When the Israelites were heading for the Promised Land, they had to do one thing for the waters to part. It was one thing keeping them from receiving what God had already promised them. They had to MOVE. God wants us to take a step, then He will open the door. We can choose to walk in faith or wander in fear. When I decided to step out of fear and post my first video on Facebook, after I finished, I was like, "Is this it?" Seriously, I believe that we can be sitting on dreams and visions that God has given us, yet we are so afraid at what the crowd might say, instead of stepping out. The Bible teaches us that, "Obedience is better than sacrifice." Is it fear of failure that keeps you complacent in the mess that you are presently in? God's will is an expression of His love. When we don't understand what God is doing, we have to have patience. God knows what's best for us. We can't see the end result, but He can. God's path may be a path of temporary pain, but all those delays, difficulties and problems are building your character. What problem, situation, relationship, job, choice or anything else that is keeping you from moving? Whatever it is, take it to God in prayer and submit it to Him. Have faith and step out. Trust me, you will be so glad you did.

"Then the Lord said to Moses, "Why are you crying out to me? Tell the Israelites to move on." Exodus 14:15

Day 7:

Celebrate the vision; but don't take the crowd

Each time God is about to do something new in your life, whether it be receiving a new anointing, going to the next level of your destiny or taking you into a season of prosperity; He will lead you into a place where the crowd will not be able to go. In Genesis 12, God told Abram to leave, to go from his familiarity. He was telling him, "you leave these things for Me and I will give these things to you." Why take extra baggage that will only get in the way? We try so hard to hold on to what makes us whole. God is saying, "let go of what you are used to."

How can you see what God has for you if you do not unleash what you are holding on to?

There are 4 kinds of people in our lives: those that add, subtract, multiply and divide. Remove the people who subtract and divide. They will slow your progress.

Everyone will not celebrate your success because they can't see what God has for you. All they know is where you have come from and how you were previously. Most people know you by your shame, instead of your name. The only issue with that, is what you answer by.

Jesus made it very clear in Matthew 5:10, "with blessings comes persecution." Certain things you have to keep to yourself. Quit trying to make people share in your dreams and visions. It was placed in you. If people decide to walk out of your life; it just means their part in your book was over. Turn the page to the next chapter. Your blessing is there.

"The Lord said to Abram, "Go from your country, your people and your father's household to the land I will show you." Genesis 12:1

Day 8: Which way

The reason why most people never hear God speak to them is that they never slow down enough to let God talk to them. Hurry is the death of prayer! You've got to slow down. You've got to be quiet. We all want to have some noise in our ear. Either listening to music, have the TV going, noise from the crowd, being on social media, etc. We pray and ask "what next," but don't listen intently for an answer from God. God will send people into your life to answer a prayer that you have prayed about so long. But if it is not what you want to hear, you ignore them. Being disobedient and not heeding the voice of the Lord, will only cause you to take the test over again. You have got to wait expectantly. Psalms 37:7 says, "Be still in the presence of the Lord, and wait patiently for him to act." NLT

We place so much focus on what is going on in the world than what is in the Word. We trust a GPS (which can get us lost), more than we trust God, who directs our paths.

If you want to know which direction to take, ask the Driver. His Word will guide you, just as it says in Psalms 119:105, "Your Word is a lamp to my feet, and a light to my path." Even when it seems so dark that you are unable to see what is ahead of you, trust that God knows exactly where you are. He has you.

"Your Word is a lamp to guide my feet and a light for my path." Psalms 119:105

Day 9: What are you thinking about?

Do you ever sit and wonder about what you are thinking of? Most of us do not, yet most sin begins in our own thought. Throughout life, we all learn that our thoughts become words; our words become actions; our actions become habits, and your habits develop your character which in turn develops your destiny. In Philippians 4:8, God's Word says, "And now, dear brothers and sisters, one final thing. Fix your thoughts on was is true, and honorable, and right, and pure, and lovely, and admirable. Think about those things that are excellent and worthy of praise." Once you choose to think positive things, positive things will happen. If you continue to think negative, negative things will find you. "As a man or woman thinketh, so is he or she." What are your thoughts about your future, family, career, friends, relationships, religion, society or finances? If you really desire to know the will of God, go and find the answer in the Word of God. There you will find His will for your life. The only truth is the Word of God. Allow God to renew your mind. Stay blessed.

"And now, dear brothers and sisters, one final thing. Fix your thoughts on what is true and honorable, and right, and pure, and lovely, and admirable. Think about things that are excellent and worthy of praise." Philippians 4:8

Day 10: The hand of Love

Discipline is not to be confused with punishment. God doesn't take pleasure in punishing us. It is a response to His eternal love. God loves you so much that He sent His only Son to die for our sins. Yet we in the comfort of our worldly desires get upset when we are going through trials, hardship, pain, tribulations, and suffering. We look at each other and wonder "what did they do?" Instead of seeing that God is doing a work in that person. I look back and realize that my hardships were all because of God building my character. God leads us through the wilderness, but He does not leave us there. He is right next to you. I thank God that He is leading me through. His discipline works for our own good. It is to glorify His name. Your faith will be stronger, and an intimate relationship will be renewed.

"Know then in your heart that as a man disciplines his son, so the Lord your God disciplines you."
Deuteronomy 8:5

Day 11: His plans leads to peace!!

You may feel as if you are walking in a dark cave. You may feel as if everything has been taken away from you. The things that may have been so easy for you in the past, is no longer doable. All the doors that you knock on are locked. You may feel as if you want to scream and cry out "why Lord?" Whatever happened to my plans? Did they just disappear? Did they die? You may feel as if the sight you were born with has just diminished. The world will show you so much, yet offer you nothing. It all hurts so badly, yet God in His splendor will not let you down.

My mind had me shut in. I felt as if I couldn't get out. No matter how far I ran, the issues, problems, and hurt were still there. I had to let it go. I can now see clearly. God has allowed me to see from His perspective and the vision is amazing. He is doing a new thing in you. Even as you read this. When you let go, God's hand is there to hold you up. Your plans are now "His plans." Let go and let God. This is the start of a new chapter for you.

"Then you will experience God's peace which exceeds anything we can understand. His peace will guard your hearts and mind as you live in Jesus Christ." Philippians 4:7

Day 12: Is God really silent?

In our walk as born-again believers, it may seem that God is silent. But God is never silent. What looks like silence and inactivity to us, is God allowing us the opportunity to listen to His "still small voice." God wants us to see the provisions that He has made for us by faith. He is involved in every area of your life—-the very hairs on your head are numbered. However, there are times when we have to walk in obedience to the light that God has already given us before He sheds more light on our path. God speaks to us through His Word. Whenever it feels as if God is not there; know that the Teacher is always silent during the test.

There may be times that you feel as if you have asked and still have not received an answer from God. Sometimes, you have to apply for the job or the house; even talking to other people who have wisdom (seeking out Godly counsel.) God speaks to us all in several different ways. So even when it feels as if He isn't saying anything, the silence could actually mean more than words.

But if he chooses to remain quiet, who can criticize him? When he hides his face, no one can find him, whether an individual or a nation. Job 34:29

Day 13: Suffering for Christ

When the sun is shining and everything going our way, we don't feel the need to run to God. But desperate times leads to desperate prayers. When we're helpless to change our situation, we cry out to our Savior who delivers us from our distress. Everything God does in our lives is for our benefit, including suffering. Though they never seem pleasant at the time, hard times produces wonderful benefits in our lives. It is the things that God does in you through the journey that will make you who you are. I remember the pain I suffered when I lost my license and my job. I felt as if all was over for me. I didn't understand that God was still working on my behalf. The things Jesus had to do during the times of His ministry here on earth, required a lot from Him, and He was perfect. So if Jesus had to go to the Father early in the morning and cry out His name and call upon Him, we have to do the same. And no matter what we see, still trust His plan and process. Because on the other side of all this pain, the "SON" is still shining.

"Dear brothers and sisters, when troubles of any kind come your way, consider it an opportunity for great joy." James 1:2

Day 14: Your Faith

Jesus touched the blind man and said, "it shall be done to you according to your faith." Such a simple phrase, yet powerful position. How much faith do you have? Faith isn't just a thought; it is an action. It is impossible to show God our faith when our fear is holding us back. The only thing that keeps us imprisoned, is our minds. We whisper "faith" through our thoughts, but we yell "fear" with our walks. We say we trust in God, who can do the impossible, but we wait for the crowd to start cheering us on before we even take the next step. Even if the process of transitioning is hard, know that God uses steps of devastation as a place of education. Step out of your comfort zone, and watch God open doors.

God has given us all a measure of faith. What or where is your faith? Who is your faith in? What is keeping you from moving forward? Make a list of things today that you need to give to God, because you may feel fear walking in them.

"Then He touched their eyes, saying, "It shall be done to you according to your faith." Matthew 9:29

Day 15: Look ahead

Our mind is a powerful thing, and your thoughts have the ability to affect your performance in every area of your life. In fact, your life cannot go forward, if your mind is going backward. Thinking and dwelling on past hurts or mistakes can actually cause us to relive the pain and prevent us from moving forward.

God says in Isaiah 43:18-19, "Do not earnestly remember the former things; neither consider the things of old. Behold I am doing a new thing." I encourage you to get your mind off your failures and disappointments and begin to look forward in your thinking. Because God is greater than your past, and He has a wonderful plan for your future. When God allowed me to practice again, I kept wondering: why does it seem as if God is taking me backward? It wasn't that He was taking me backward, He was actually doing a "NEW" thing in me. Doing it your way may not have worked, but placing God as the Source and acknowledging Him in all of your ways, you are destined to pass the test this time. What things in your life is causing you to not look ahead? What is taking your focus off of moving? What is keeping you stuck in the familiar? Whatever it is, lay it at His feet, ask Him, seek out various opportunities and knock on the door. See if He will open it up for you.

"No, dear brothers and sisters, I have not achieved it, but I focus on this one thing: Forgetting the past and looking forward to what lies ahead." Philippians 3:13

Day 16: Letting go of what's behind

Why do we hold on to the things that are gone, relationships that didn't work out, the times when other people hurt us, disappointments in our lives, missed opportunities and so much more? We cause hurt, pain and bitterness just by our thoughts of "what if?" We keep looking back at what we were, what we had; instead of trying to allow God to show us who we are. Letting go of the past, opens doors to some amazing blessings. I chose to let go of who I was, to become who God wanted me to be. There is a purpose in everything.

Jesus said in Luke 17:32, "Remember what happened to Lot's wife." Stop gazing at what is behind. Stop trying to carry everything with you when God has new plans for you. The world has made us feel as "what we have, is who we are." They put a title on everything. And we tend to believe our "title" is who we are. When the true "WHO" is already within you. Every time we go back to the pain of our past we are just re-opening a wound that God is trying to heal. When the past tempts you to look back, learn from Lot's wife, and keep looking ahead into the place that God is leading you to next. Today, choose not to be captive of what you once was.

"But Lot's wife looked back as she was following behind him, and she turned into a pillar of salt." Genesis 19:26

Day 17: Keep Sowing

In the book of Genesis, in the very beginning, God established a system of increase. Everything in life operates off of SeedTime and Harvest. We all have seeds within us. The only issue is that we don't have the patience for the allotted time. Whenever a farmer or gardener plant a seed, it takes time to grow. There are seeds of success, provision, and increase inside of you. As long as you have seed, you have an increase in your hand. But a seed will lay dormant until it is placed in the right condition. Sow your seed into fertile (good) ground. You have to plant the seed and water it, in order for it to grow. God also sends people into your lives at the right time to water what is already inside of you. Ultimately it is Him, who will give the increase. What seeds do you have in your hands? Seeds can be as simple as the seed of a smile that will produce happiness in your life. It can be a financial seed that will produce prosperity into your life.

Whatever you have, give, and it shall be given back to you in greater measures.

The Bible says the God's Word is water, and when you speak the Word of God, you are watering your seeds. Ask the Lord today to show you what seeds you have in your hand. Ask Him to show you where to plant them. Then step out and sow because He will watch over those seeds to produce an abundant harvest in every area of your life. "While the earth remains, Seedtime and harvest, And cold and heat, And summer and winter, And day and night shall not cease." Genesis 8:22

Day 18: We can't do it alone

As a new follower of Christ, I thought things would be so much easier. I assumed things would be smoother and I wouldn't have to work as hard, because I was now a "Christian." I was totally wrong; I didn't know that things would actually get harder, more trying, more persecutions. I didn't know that I would walk out of one wilderness, just to go to another one. Most of us want the crown, yet we do not want to have to carry the cross. There were nights I would sit and ask God, "why," and "what next," but I still did not get answers. Or at least the answers I was looking for. I was receiving convictions, yet I ignored them as "it is just my own thought." Was it because God was speaking and I wasn't listening? Probably because I was still talking. And probably because I didn't want to do His will, just wanted Him to bless my will that I had planned and put together. I kept trying so hard to do right, to live right, to act right, to pray right. When in actuality, I was missing out on the most important task: LISTENING. I honestly thought I could do it alone. All those nights of crying and shedding so many tears, just because I didn't want to hear any negativity from anyone else. Sometimes we are so tied up in our own lie, that we do not want anyone to call us out. Because it just may be true.

In so many different places in the Bible, God always used pairs. Even with the animal, He sent them in pairs. In Mark 6:7, after He called the twelve disciples together, He started sending them out "two by two." God has gifted us all with so many gifts and talents, but none of them to include "doing it alone." One of my many gifts include exhortation. But as much as I love to encourage, I can honestly say, I need it more. Sometimes we may start to feel empty, but God does desire for us to come to Him alone and refuel. Even if it isn't saying a Word, He knows your heart. And He just wants to connect with His beloved son or daughter.

This is a prayer that I said to God once I decided to surrender it all to Him. Even if you may feel as if you can't surrender it all to Him, because you may not be ready, He is truly ready to receive you just as you are. We will never be "ready enough" to go to God. We can never get ourselves together or be "clean" enough. Nothing you do will ever make God feel any different about you. He is Love.

Father,
I come to you as your child, thanking you for calling me. I ask, in the name of Jesus, to open my eyes and ears, Lord, to hear your direction and guidance. Father, you never intended for us to do it all by ourselves. Your Word says in Ecclesiastes 4:12 says, "A person standing alone can be attacked and defeated, but two can stand back to back and conquer. Three are even better, for a triple-braided cord is not easily broken." Help me, Father, to not push away anyone that you have placed alongside me for this season. In Jesus name. Amen

"Though one may be overpowered by another, two can withstand him. And a threefold cord is not quickly broken." Ecclesiastes 4:12

"When we get together, I want to encourage you in your faith, but I also want to be encouraged by you." Romans 1:12

Day 19: You can move your mountain

What mountain are you choosing to stay at? What problems in your life continues to bother you? What addiction do you feel is overtaking your life? What financial hardship keeps coming up? What relationship are you staying in that isn't going anywhere? What is causing all of your hurt and pain? Sometimes, we are the cause of our own mountains. Yet, God has given us the power to move it. God said, if we had the faith of a mustard seed, we could move mountains. Look at the mountain in front of you. When it becomes too big for you to move, speak to it. Submit it to God. You have to make a choice to stop going around the same old mountain year after year. Every day, we are given test. It could be in answering a phone call from a debtor, just so that God can deal with you financially. It could be in deciding to clean your apartment, so that God can see if He can even trust you with the bigger things, like owning your own home. It could be in staying at that job, where everyone seems to belittle you and treat you differently, it could be to prepare you to be promoted to a position you don't even qualify for or even owning the company. We do not know all the answers, yet God places scenarios right in front of our face every single day. Choose today, to not keep taking the same test over and over. Your elevation could be right around the corner.

"I tell you the truth, you can say to this mountain," may you be lifted up and thrown into the sea," and it will happen. But you must really believe it will happen and have no doubt in your heart. Mark 11:23

Day 20: The witness of the Spirit

The witness of the Spirit in our heart is our most precious possession. It is the key to the treasure-house, for by that witness, we know God and have the assurance of eternal life.

The witness is not an audible voice, but it is a quiet certainty. It is so quiet that it can easily be ignored, but it is so clear and persistent that we can only ignore it by willful neglect or rebellion. The witness of the Spirit is an inner quiet joy, but if we stray from the Father's will, a cloud darkens our life, and we feel grief of heart that all is not well. This is the grief of the Spirit, and it is good that we feel it. Just as we feel pain if we get too close to the fire, and so are saved from harm, so too we feel inner grief if we stray from Father's will.

The witness of the Spirit is the mean by which we are alerted to the fact that there is danger. Guard the witness. If your heart says stop, then stop and wait on God. We cannot live by logic; we live by our relationship with God, and the foundation of that is the witness of the Holy

Spirit. Commune with God and the witness is refreshed and renewed, and your joy of salvation rises like a fountain.

"For his Spirit joins with our spirit to affirm that we are God's children." Romans 8:16

Day 21: Losing Jesus

How astonishing that Jesus', mother and stepfather could have overlooked Him for a whole day! But then they missed Him, and set off to search for Him. They overlooked Him because they assumed they knew all about Him; their hearts were not troubled, and they assumed He was where He should be. So they continued in their daily routine for a day before they missed Him. Then they began searching, and they spent three whole days without understanding how and where they should find Him.

How long can we continue in our daily routine, even of prayer and Bible reading, before we suddenly sense that He is not in it in an unmistakeable way? Suddenly, we long for Him. This is a sign of love, for it is only those who love Jesus who miss His presence. We ache for that something that only His presence can supply. This is not the aching sense of lostness that engulfs the sinner-it is the ache of a heart that longs for the loving touch and affirmation of our great Friend.

There is no word to describe Him; He is closer than a friend, yet He is Master too. He is majesty in His authority, and yet He washes our feet with a positive kindness that does not shame us, but makes us believe we can be like Him.

Come, Lord Jesus, I long for you.

"because they assumed he was among the other traveler. But when he didn't show up that evening, they started looking for him among their relatives and friends. When they couldn't find him, they went back to Jerusalem to search for him there. Three days later they finally discovered him in the Temple, sitting among the religious teachers, listening to them and asking questions." Luke 2

Day 22: Circling your mountains

In Deuteronomy 2:1, God had told Moses to tell the people "you have wandered around this mountain long enough, turn and go North." The Israelites wandered for so long in the wilderness that they became used to it. A journey that should have taken 11 days, took 40 years. We also go around the same mountain without making any progress for the best life God has given us.

What exactly does it take for you to leave the mountain that you have created? How long do you plan on wandering around your own iniquities? What family member or friend do we need to hear from to tell us "it is ok now to leave?" God speaks directly to each one of us regarding our lives. You create a mess, pray about it, but stay in it. When God is continually speaking and saying "you have been here long enough," it is truly time for you to move.

Job loss- God says "I have better, Go this way." Proverbs 16:9

Relationships fall apart- God says "I have better. This is who I chose for you." Proverbs 31:10

Financial issues-God says "I will supply all of your needs according to my riches and glory in Christ Jesus." Phil 4:9

God tests all of our hearts, and we will take the same test over and over again until we pass it. He will take as much time as needed to get all of the junk out of our hearts when we let Him.

When God says "move" then you should move. Don't turn to others and tell them when you plan to move. Just GO, and He will tell you which direction. Even if you are not able to see a way out, He is the Light that directs your steps. Trust His guidance and not everyone else's opinions. Leave that mountain. Don't die wandering in the wilderness. Stay blessed.

Day 23: Parenting: Taking Care

Is it possible that in an effort to be the best parent you can be, you sometimes neglect your own spiritual growth? When the demands of your family require you to be on the go from dawn until late at night, you may be tempted to sacrifice your quiet time, prayer or other spiritual disciplines. Paul recognized this tendency in the people he was disciplined and cautioned against it. You will have a hard time giving to anyone from an empty spiritual "cup." Even Jesus had to take time away from the crowds and His disciples to talk to the Father.

When we forget to give God the best of our day, we may begin to see issues like anger, bitterness, resentment, and moral dilemmas arise. We are not doing our kids any favors when we are spiritually exhausted. As Paul was saying goodbye to the Ephesians elders, he cautioned them, "keep watch over yourselves and all the flock of which the Holy Spirit has made you oversee." (Acts 20:28 NIV). Notice he warned them first to keep watch over themselves; then their flock. What a valuable lesson for us as parents.

When your relationship with God is your first priority, you are in a better position to serve others and your family.

"If you think you are standing strong, be careful not to fall." 1 Corinthians 10:12

Day 24: A heart of passion

Another word for heart is passion. There are certain subjects that you feel deeply passionate about and others that you could care less about. Some experiences turn you on and capture your attention, while others turn you off or bore you to tears. These reveal the nature of your heart, so listen for inner promptings that point to the ministry God intends for you to have.

When you were growing up, you may have discovered that you were intensely interested in some subjects that no one else in the family cared about. Where did those interest come from? They came from God!

God had a purpose in giving you these inborn interest. Your emotional heartbeat is a key to understanding your shape for service. Don't ignore your interest; consider how they might be used for God's glory. There is a reason that you love to do those things. Listen to your heart.

What are some things that you are truly passionate about? Take them to God and ask Him to show you and lead you into the direction He desires for you to take. In doing this, you will experience a sense of peace in every assignment He sends you. Ultimately, He will lead you into the purpose that He placed you here for. It will lead towards your destiny.

"As a face is reflected in water, so the heart reflects the real person." Proverbs 27:19

Day 25: Always be joyful

Even when you are hurting, always be joyful. Even when you don't see a way out, always be joyful. Even when you do not see a way to get the money to pay the bill, always be joyful. Even if you lose your home or car, always be joyful. Even if you lose your job, always be joyful. Even if you have been abused, always be joyful. Even if you feel alone, always be joyful.

This list could go on and on with, "but what if?" It was like the Lord knew there would be so much in our lives that we would have to deal with, that would take our joy away. And immediately after He said this, he said, "never stop praying." 1 Thessalonians 5:17. There were times I would be speaking to others, and I would tell them, "no one can take your joy, that is something you give away." Yet it so easy to say, but so hard to do. "Christ came to give us life and give it more abundantly." John 10:10

The only that blocks you from enjoying your life, is you. When you are faced with a situation that seems like it is tough, take it to Jesus Christ. He will give you the peace that passes all understanding. Pray this prayer.

Father, I acknowledge your presence with me at this very moment. You alone Lord know everything that I will face in this day. Lord, I ask that when I am hurting and don't know what to do, that You speak to my heart. Remind me of your promise to me. Allow your love to work through me, even when the other person has caused me so much pain. Allow me to see past my own selfish ways and love them even more, just as Christ loves me. In Jesus name. Amen

"Always be joyful. Never stop praying." 1 Thessalonians 5:16-17

Day 26: Divining Purposes

We look at trials as the worse things that could happen in our lives. Most of us just don't understand "why" God could or would allow certain things to happen. In His Word, God says "be truly glad, there is wonderful joy ahead, even though you must endure many trials for a little while."

God has placed in each one of us a divine purpose. He allows things to happen, so that He can bring to surface those things we need to deal with, to test our faith or test our devotion to Him. He will bring to surface any unforgiveness, bitterness, hatred, jealousy, idolatry, or anything else that is not of Him. The things that are causing damage to ourselves, others and our relationship to Him.

Pain should get everyone's attention. Although most of us tend to ignore that pain for a while, until it is too hard to bear. God will continue to send messages to you saying, "you have to deal with this problem My child." If you are a child of God, trust that you will be disciplined. Take the issue to God, go to His Word and He will speak to your heart and heal any pain and hurt you have. The pain is temporary; His promises are eternal. No matter what you may be dealing with today, trust that your Heavenly Father desires to direct your path.

"So be truly glad. There is wonderful joy ahead, even though you must endure many trials for a little while. These trials will show that your faith is genuine. It is being tested as fire test and purifies gold though your faith is far more precious than mere gold. So when your faith remains strong through many trials, it will bring you much praise and glory and honor on the day when Jesus Christ is revealed to the whole world." 1 Peter 1:6-7

Day 27: Farming

A farmer is one who plants the seeds, waters it routinely and waits for a season or so for the crops to grow. We as children of God work in the same exact manner. As we study God's Word, a seed is planted in our heart. Whenever we are going through a particular circumstance or situation, that seed will surface and grow within you. Most times, just through struggling, trusting God and continuing to focus on Him, the seed is growing.

In 1 Corinthians 3:6 Paul says, "I planted the seed in your hearts, and Apollos watered it, but it was God who made it grow."

I remember when I was a new believer, I felt it was my duty to fix my family. I would quote scriptures and play nothing but church music and sermons just so that they could hear. It wasn't my place to fix them. It was my place to receive my growth process. This is called spiritual pride. I was actually doing opposite of what my plan was. As believers, we tend to try within our own strength to fix someone or force our faith on them. Our families, friends, co-workers, etc. All you have to do is plant the seed, someone else will water it, but ultimately it is God who will give the increase. We cannot fix what God has created. We have to allow Him to do the molding.

"I planted the seed in your hearts, and Apollos watered it, but it was God who made it grow. It's not important who does the planting, or who does the watering. What's important is that God makes the seed grow.' 1 Corinthians 3:6-7

Day 28: Quiet Time

There is so much going on in the world that sometimes we have to get away to a place alone with Jesus. The disciples had come back from their tour and told Jesus all they had done. Jesus replied, "Let's go off by ourselves to a quiet place and rest a while." He had said this because there were so many people coming and going that they didn't have time to eat.

There are times when it seems as if everything is going wrong, your just moving and don't know which direction to go in, things are falling apart, and everyone is bringing their issues and problems to you. There is a reason Christ said, "get away by ourselves to a quiet place." Do not allow personal problems, social media, frustrations of the world, family issues or anything else to get in the way of receiving your feeding form the Word. Even if it is outside first thing in the morning, in your closet or bathroom, in your car before heading to your job or anywhere else. It is in that time that Jesus will refuel you with what you need to keep going. Do not be a car driving on an almost empty tank because you will not get far without running out of gas.

"The apostles gathered around Jesus and reported to him all they had done and taught. Then, because so many people were coming and going that they didn't even have a chance to eat, he said to them, "Come with me by yourself to a quiet place and get some rest." So they went away by themselves in a bot to a solitary place." Mark 6:30-32

Day 29: Do not go by what you see

"For we walk by faith, not by sight." The first thing we do when waking up in the morning is opening our eyes. It normally takes a while for our eyes to focus on light since for hours we have been in the darkness. Our mind is still asleep. Not knowing what God has planned for the day, we place our trust in our vision. We ask God to lead us, while looking for ways to just "figure it all out" ourselves.

As a new believer, recently I had been saying, "God, I feel like my life is at a standstill." I felt distant, I felt alone, I felt like no matter what I did, nothing was working. Sitting in my quiet time with the Lord, I just kept hearing, "do not go by what you see." I had been judging situations of failure, oppositions, obstacles and the trials on what I was seeing. I would pray to God, then go to google for an answer. I kept looking and waiting for an answer. When the answer had already been revealed to me.

God's Word says, "trust in the Lord with all of your heart and do not lean to your own understanding." Proverbs 3:5. Yet we lean to what we see and hear. God is our Creator, Alpha, and Omega, Beginning and the End. He is the Author of our own individual lives. He knows every hair on your head, Luke 12:7. If you are dealing with tough times at this present moment, take it to God and ask Him to open your spiritual eyes. Ask Him to show you Jesus Christ in everything that you see.

Pray that God will allow the Holy Spirit to lead and guide you in the way that you should go. Because if you continue to go by what you see; your eyes will fail you every time.

"Your Word is a lamp to my feet and a light to my path." Psalms 119:105

Day 30: Which way?

Do you know which way to go? Maybe you are facing an important decision in your job, at home or in your relationships. Know this: God, will teach you what you should do. He promises to show you the path you should take. He is watching over you and giving you advice every step of the way.

God is not just concerned with the goal, or end result. It is not just getting you from point "a" to point "b." He is not only with you, but the Bible says that the steps of a good man are ordered by the Lord. He actually orders your steps. Even on today, your steps have been ordered. So if it seems as if you are just walking and do not know what is going on in your life, or feel as if things are becoming so chaotic, know at this very moment, God is guiding you in the direction you need to go. Sometimes the way God takes us could seem like it doesn't make sense. But God's ways are higher than our ways. We can never imagine that the Creator has His eyes on you; even at this very moment. While you are sitting here reading this, God led you here. Whatever you have within yourself that you do not want to give to God, He is saying "let it go." Trust Him, and He will direct your path.

The Lord says, "I will guide you along the best pathway for your life. I will advise you and watch over you." Psalms 32:8

"O Lord, I know the way of man is not in himself; it is not in man who walks to direct his own steps." Jeremiah 10:23

Day 31: Agape Love

Love is such a powerful word. Yet we say it so easily but show it so horribly. Everything about God is love. He sent His one and only Son to die for our sins. 1 John 4:10. That's agape love. He has given us the opportunity to live an eternal life through His Son Jesus Christ. God's love is personal. He knows each of us individually and loves each of us personally. He is a mighty love that has no beginning and no end. It is this experiencing of God's love that distinguishes Christianity from all other religions. Why does God love us? It is because of who He is: "God is Love."

Pray this prayer with me:

Father,
Every moment of the day, you continue to show me how much you love me. In my natural body, dealing with so many emotions, I may not show my love as much as I

express it. Father, help me to love the way you love. Help me to show compassionate love to everyone. To not just say, but show it. I pray for anyone that is hurting and doesn't feel loved. I ask Father that you lavish them with your unconditional agape love. In Jesus name I ask and pray.
Amen

"This is real love-not the we loved God, but the he loved us and sent his Son as a sacrifice to take away our sins. Dear friends, since God loved us that much, we surely ought to love each other. No one has ever seen God. But if we love each other, God lives in us, and his love is brought to full expression in us." 1 John 4:10-12

"For God so loved the world that He gave His only begotten Son, that whoever believes in Him should not perish but have everlasting life." John 3:16

Day 32: Your Words

The words we speak affect others. Words can make people want to be near us or want to run and hide from us. While positive, constructive, and productive comments build others up and please God, negative and destructive words tear down and dishonor God.

We get provoked or irritated, and we reach without a filter. We share opinions that are flesh-led instead of Spirit-led. We suck the air out of the room with tones of disgust, anger, disapproval, or sarcasm. We give the look. We talk about other people, bend the truth, and point fingers. Ungodly talk can weaken relationships to frailty, and is as offensive to the Lord as stinky, sour milk is to us. Until we identify the destructive words we speak and expel them from our vocabulary, our conversations will continue to stink, and we will not experience the love, joy, peace in our homes and relationships that we long for.

Ask God to heal your heart from anger, hatred, bitterness, unforgiveness, jealousy or anything that is causing you to lash out at others. Not only does it corrupt your heart and soul, but it also tears down the other person heart as well. Words you say to a person will be with them forever. As most of us have been taught as a child, "If you don't have anything nice to say, then don't say nothing at all."

"A quarrelsome person starts fights as easily as hot embers light charcoal or fire lights wood." Proverbs 26:21

"Death and life are in the power of the tongue, And those who love it will eat its fruit." Proverbs 18:21

Day 33: Ownership vs Stewardship

Much of the heartache we experience in life stems from loss. Loss of a job, loss of a loved one, loss of a home, loss of a relationship or anything that is of importance to you. If you understood that it was never ours to begin with, it would lessen the blow.

When we lose anything that we were so very much attached to, we grieve. When we receive anything that is new, i.e., a house, a car, a new relationship, a job, we rejoice. Do you sometimes start to praise the gift rather than the Giver? Anything that was given or taken, it all belonged to God who gave it in the first place. Sometimes, God will give us what we prayed for so long and hard for, just to let you know, it isn't what you needed in the first place. He gives, and He takes away, yet we only receive happiness and joy over what we perceive is good in our eyes. Realize that joy should also come from the things God removes out of our lives as well. He loves you so much to remove that "thing or person" out of the way, to give you His absolute best. Maybe you have experienced some loss in your life that has been hard to get past. Holding on to that thing or person, only slows down the process. If you had to have it to get to your next level in life, God wouldn't have removed it from you. Even those materialistic possessions that God gives us, is because He desires to give us bigger and better. Yet He tests us to see how we take care of the small things before He gives us the bigger. If you are praying for a financial blessing, and you have a job, are you being a good steward of the "small" income that you have now? Why would God give you 1000's when you can't even budget with the 100's? Most people will not know how to handle the big thing that God has to already given them. That is why the word says, "For everyone to whom much is given, much more is required.' Luke 12:48

"Yours, O Lord, is the greatness, the power, the glory, the victory, and the majesty. Everything in the heavens and on earth is yours, O Lord, and this is your kingdom. We adore you as the one who is over all things."1 Chronicles 29:11

Day 34: We are in it together

Apologizing is hard work. Apologizing and changing your behavior is even harder, and what makes it so hard is pride. Dating and marriage always to some degree involve each person struggling for control. When your behaviors are driven by pride, you want to win every argument, always be right, see difficulties as your partner's fault, bring up your partners admitted failures of the past, and explain away or deny your own sins and weaknesses.

You need other people's input and critique to know how you sound, how you look, how your actions affect other people. In humility, realize that you aren't quite as brilliant and infallible as you think you are. "Do not think of yourself more highly than you ought, but rather think of yourself with sober judgment, in accordance with the faith God has distributed to each of you" (Romans 12:3).

When your spouse has an issue with something you've said or done, listen twice and think three times before you say anything. It may just be that the best thing you can say is, "I'm sorry."

"Because of the privilege and authority God has given me, I give each of you this warning: Don't think you are better than you really are. Be honest in your evaluation of yourself, measuring yourselves by the faith God has given us." Romans 12:3

Day 35: Keeping your eyes on Christ

As we turn on the news, we see nothing but evilness in this world that we reside in. In my growth, I have attempted to distance myself from watching the news, social media or anything else that doesn't allow me to grow in Christ. Yet, the more I hear about what is going on, I have to realize that this is the life we have right now. We are temporary residents in this world (1 Peter 1:17)

The enemy is the ruler of this world, yet Jesus Christ has conquered it all. "We know that we are children of God and that this world around us is under the control of the evil one." 1 John 5:19 NLT.

This battle has already been won. Anyone that is separated from God lives in a hopeless place.

Keeping your eyes on Jesus even during these times of sadness, wars, hardship or any other personal suffering, will give you so much joy. Just knowing that we mourn now, to laugh later Even as Christians, we cannot love perfectly, nor can we hate perfectly. (i.e., without malice).

His Word says "You have heard that it was said, "You shall love your neighbor and hate your enemy. But I say to you, love your enemies and pray for those who persecute you." Matthew 5:43-44. As long as we live in this world, we will have trouble. But if we keep our eyes on Jesus Christ, the Author, and Finisher of our faith, we will rejoice in eternity. Trust in Him and believe that what He said, He will be faithful to do.

"We know that we are the children of God and that the world around us is under the control of the evil one. " 1 John 5:19

Day 36: Small Beginnings

Have an attitude of gratitude and do not despise small beginnings, for God could be testing your character. It's not all about the small things that we see. It's our "attitude" about the things we see. We are praying about big things when God is taking us in the process of loving the little things.

You are praying about the big house when God has given you a small apartment to care for. You are praying about graduating from college when God has allowed you to pass your first semester. You are praying about a brand new car when God has allowed someone to bless you with their old car. You are praying for a new job when God has opened the door for you at a minimum wage job. You are praying for a financial breakthrough when God has blessed you with a $.50 raise at your current job. He is able to accelerate you exactly where you are. It is God who opens and closes doors. The Bible says, "you will reap in due season if you don't give up." Galatians 6:9

We pray; He answers. What we see is temporal. What Jesus has given you is eternal. Be grateful for the little things, and watch how God will manifest the big things in your life. God is the master of the "little things" as well as the "big things." It is the small things that open the door. Have mustard seed faith for "all things."

"Do not despise these small beginnings, for the Lord rejoices to see the work begin, to see the plumb line in Zerubbabel's hand." (The seven lamps represent the eyes of the Lord that search all around the world.) Zechariah 4:6

Day 37: Worldly Desires

In this scripture, James says, "You want what you don't have, so you scheme and kill to get it. You are jealous of what others have, but you can't get it, so you fight and wage war to take it away from them. Yet you do not have what you want because you do not ask God for it. And even when you ask, you don't get it because your motives are all wrong-you want only what will give you pleasure." James 4:2-3, NLT.

As I sit here and listen to people saying what they would do, "if I won the lottery" makes me wonder, Is this one of the reasons WHY Jesus made this statement? He wants us to be blessed with all that He offers, not what the world offers. He changes the way we see things as we are renewed. In Romans 12:2 He says, "Don't copy the behaviors and customs of the world, but let God transform you into a new person by changing the way you think. Then you will learn to know God's will for you, which is good and pleasing and perfect."

We don't know what most people kneel down and pray for. Winning the lottery could be a blessing or a curse. Even the enemy know what your desires are only because we speak them out. It all depends on our motives. "I want to buy a bigger house, I want to stop working, go on a vacation or even get the car of my dreams." What about giving to the poor, opening a shelter for the homeless, starting a nonprofit for people who cannot afford healthcare or medications, or even starting a business for those who need a second chance. Grace and mercy is given to us every single day. Yet we look at our own selfish desires and not Godly desires. Will your desires actually glorify God or give praise to you?

Yes, a lot of us want to be rich, but only God knows our heart and motives. This world has become so carnally selfish, that majority people have closed their ears and heart to the cries of the poor, broken, widowed, hurt, those in captivity or even the cries of the children. What are your true desires? Is it for you or for others?

"Do not love the world or the things in the world. If anyone loves the world, the love of the Father is not in him. For all that is in the world - the desires of the flesh and the desires of the eyes and pride in possessions - is not from the Father but is from the world. And the world is passing away along with its desires, but whoever does the will of God abides forever." 1 John 15-17

Day 38: It will pay off in time

Just because a situation looks gloomy doesn't mean it's over. It will all pay off after a while. Don't lose focus, faith or heart. Have hope in Jesus.

1.) Learn to be patient and wait on God. There are times where God allowed me to face adversity to see if I'm ready for what He has for me. "Weeping may endure for a night, but joy comes in the morning." There is a time to stop crying over the past, give praise in the present and press on to the future.

2.) I can't operate in the "now," I have to operate in the future out of faith.

3.) I must understand WHO is telling me things will get better, WHO has promised me abundant life. Don't allow others to distract you. Everyone may not see that dream that God has placed in you. God may have you going through a temporary season of hardship, for the permanent blessing of Heaven. That is the grace of God.

4.) For things to get better, I must do what the Lord says. Restrain from weeping and hold back my tears. Don't waste another tear on that situation.

Weeping is allowing my actions to draw attention to my situation. Only God can revive what is dead. Yet, we can speak life over those dead bones!!

The Lord says stop weeping and hold back your tears because your work will be rewarded. But rewards don't come early. They come when we are ready. Be patient, but don't just sit. Work, because the work will be rewarded. Don't stay in the rut. Rewards don't come without effort. No struggle, no success. No action, no results. It won't be easy, and it won't come fast. But you have to be willing to do what it takes.

5.) Rewards come with an attitude of expectancy. Expect a blessing and watch how God works.

Day 39: What do you do with your time?

What do you do with your time? Most people wake up to the exact same thing they did yesterday. We are so set on "sameness." What was a blessing yesterday, could turn out to be a curse today depending on how you set your focus. What or who gets the most of your time? Family, job, social media, church, significant other, friends, yourself, etc. God's plan is meant for good and not for evil for your life. Yet, we sit and wait for that plan to happen. Hoping that it will just fall into our laps. Saying things like, "I want to work at this particular company, yet won't even go to the library to fill out an application." "I want to be debt free, yet continues to buy every new style of shoe that comes out." "I want a new house, but won't even take care to clean up the small apt you have."

At the beginning of every New Year, majority people have this New Year Resolution that they do. What happened to doing a new day's resolution? If you don't change the things you did last season, you will bring them with you into your next season. Have a different perspective. We have all been blessed with the same 24 hours in a day. If you are feeling a nudge or tug to go in a different direction, that could be the Holy Spirit telling you to walk that way. Write the book, apply for the job, go on a date, move to another state, go to the gym, and accept the speaking engagement.

The time could be NOW! For no one knows what tomorrow will bring.

"For everything, there is a season, a time for every activity under heaven. A time to be born and a time to die. A time to plant and a time to harvest. A time to kill and a time to heal. A time to tear down and a time to build up. A time to cry and a time to laugh. A time to grieve and a time to dance. A time to scatter stones and a time to gather stones. A time to embrace and a time to turn away. A time to search and a time to quit searching. A time to keep and a time to throw away. A time to tear and a time to mend. A time to be quiet and a time to speak. A time to love and a time to hate. A time for war and a time for peace." Ecclesiastes 3:1-8

Day 40: Think before you act

Apologizing can be a hard thing to do. And changing your behavior can be even harder to do. Pride is what makes it so hard to get past. Dating and marriage always to some degree involve each person struggling for control. When your behaviors are driven by pride, you want to win every argument, always be right, see difficulties as your partner's fault, bring up your partner's admitted failures of the past, and explain away or deny your own sins and weaknesses.

You need other people's input and critique to know how you sound, how you look, how your actions affect other people. In humility, realize that you aren't quite as brilliant and infallible as you think you are: "Do not think of yourself more highly than you ought, but rather think of yourself with sober judgment, in accordance with the faith God has distributed to each of you" (Romans 12:3.)

When your spouse has an issue with something you've said or done, listen twice and think three times before you say anything. It may just be that the best thing you can say is, "I'm sorry."

"Because of the privilege and authority God has given me, I give each of you this warning: Don't think you are better than you really are. Be honest in your evaluation of yourselves, measuring yourselves by the faith God has given us." Romans 12:3

Day 41: Faith that is Alive

Did you know that faith can be alive or dead? Dead faith doesn't do anything. There are a lot of people who love God, but they aren't overcoming obstacles or accomplishing their God-given dreams simply because they are not putting any action behind their faith. Their faith is simply dead.

What can you do today to keep your faith alive? It doesn't have to be something big. By simply obeying God's Word and doing your best, you are keeping your fight alive. When you go to work every day and give it 100%, you are demonstrating your faith. Sometimes just putting a smile on your face when you feel discouraged is putting action behind your faith. Taking the time to go to church-that is faith that is alive. That is also faith that activates God's power. That is also faith that opens doors for God to one on your behalf! With faith that is alive, you'll rise up higher. You'll overcome obstacles, and you will move forward into the blessing and victory God has in store for you.

"But do you want to know, O foolish man, that faith without works is dead?" James 2:20

Day 42: Running from God's Will

Jonah ran from the will of God to a different place. A place that he thought would be more comfortable. He had yet to realize his disobedience, rebellion, and resistance would bring him back to that place he had run from.

God always has a plan for your life. In Jeremiah 29:11, God says, "For I know the plans that I have for you, they are plans of good and not of evil. Plans to give you a future and a hope." His will for each of us is to bring glory and honor to His name. Our stay isn't about us; it is for someone else.

The hardships, struggles, and problems that you run from only allow you to create another storm in your life. Our oppositions could be our greatest opportunities. Yet, our fear causes us to faint. Allow God to direct your path today, even if it doesn't make sense to you. His direction is so much between than our direction. Stop trying to take shortcuts along the way and just let the Holy Spirit lead you.

No matter what detours you attempt to make, God will get you where you are destined to be.

"For I know the plans I have for you," says the Lord. "They are plans for good and not for disaster, to give you a future and a hope." Jeremiah 29:11

Day 43: Consider your inspiration

The level of your dream determines the level of your inspiration. And anytime the level of your inspiration exceeds those around you, you will experience loss. Because you cannot successfully be with people who cannot dream like you dream. You will end up losing your inspiration, trying to accommodate for their lack of inspiration. One of the greatest success is staying inspired. And you have to surround yourself with people that will feed your creativity, in order to stay focused on your goals.

On the road to destiny, there are always casualties. You have to be so committed and inspired by your goals and purpose to continue on the road to destiny. Destiny is God's responsibility; He decides what you are meant to be and do in this world. But how you fulfill it, is your responsibility. You have to be able to cut the toxic relationship that does not support your destiny. Any relationship that doesn't help you grow, is a roadblock to your destination. The growth in you is predicted by the people you are willing to let go.

In order to be a true child of destiny, your desire to be what you were created to be must exceed your desire to be accepted. If acceptance is the goal, compromise is the result. If we live our lives trying to be accepted by people, we never live for ourselves. We will always make decisions based on the opinions of others. And the problem with that is if you base all of your decisions off of someone else's opinion, you'll end up helping them reach their destiny while aborting your own.

In order to effectively walk in your destiny, you have to become okay with people leaving. If they can leave your life, it is a sign they were never meant to stay. Them leaving a manifestation of your destiny. Destiny reveals the true nature of those around you. Your responsibility is to receive what destiny has been revealed!!

"These people left our churches, but they never really belonged with us; otherwise they would have stayed with us. When they left, it proved that they did not belong with us." 1 John 2:19

Day 44: Faith without works is dead

Are you waiting for God to do something in your life? One thing I've learned is that waiting should not be a passive thing. When we're waiting the correct way, we're on the lookout that God is about to pour rain on us. He is about to send His blessing our way. We talk like what we are believing for is going to happen. We act like it has already happened. We're making preparation to just walk in that thing.

It's just like when you're expecting someone for dinner; you don't wait until they show up before you decide to start cooking. Most likely you start early in the day. You make sure the house is clean, you go to the grocery store, and maybe buy some flowers for the table. You make preparations because you're expecting someone. Well, that's the attitude we need to have while we're waiting for God's promises to come to pass. As you put actions behind your prayers, your faith comes alive and opens the door for God to move mightily on your behalf.

A prayer for today "Father, I choose to put actions behind my faith today. I trust that You are at work in my life. I will with the right way-with expectancy knowing that You are leading me into the path You have for me in Jesus' name! Amen

"How foolish! Can't you see that faith without good deeds is useless?" James 2:20

Day 45: We all fall short

When we find ourselves projecting our lives on our kids, we need to look instead to our heavenly Father's display of value for us. He cashed in His Son, Jesus, to get us a pathway back to Him. Our value is in a kid, but it's not our kid; it's God's one and only Son, Jesus. God doesn't love us because of something we did for Him. He showed us His love through someone He gave for us. First, we need to linger here to discover our true sense of identity. Then as parents, let's follow God's model and sacrifice the things we love, to set our children free from: the prison of living to please. Our offsprings should be motivated by our momentum, not halted by our hangups.

Our children attempt to do all that they can to please us. Sometimes, their rebellion isn't because they desired that, it could be that they wanted more attention from mom or dad. As parents, we tend to do our best, but when our best isn't enough, we give up and just throw in the towel. God's word tells us to "train up a child in the way that he or she should go, and when they get older, they will not depart from it." Teach them about finances, credit, family, marriage, life and anything else that they will need in this world. We can't place all of our trust in allowing teachers to show them everything. That is our jobs as parents.

"For everyone has sinned; we all fall short of God's glorious standard." Roman 3:23

Day 46: Share your story

Someone else's breakthrough could be in you sharing your story. We are so quick to try and cover up and hide who we really are, that we forget who we are, that we forget about our own walk. We care so much about others opinion of us that we hide in our shame and guilt. We place focus on what looks good to society or our own eyes that we drown our pain. Our blessing could be in releasing that side of us that is covered up or hidden. It is only causing hurt to you. Stop comparing your lives to others who are also pretending. Don't just quote scripture out of the Bible, when the blessing could be in someone hearing your story. That alone could bring them to Christ!! Allow them to see what God has done for you; that will bring glory to our Heavenly Father.

Be grateful with who you are; be grateful with your own success; be grateful for hardship, because that is what causes endurance. Open up and let others be blessed by your story; because it is not just about you. It's about others that are about to go through, going through or on the way out. Don't go at it alone. Allow your story to be a blessing for you and a testimony for them.

"The woman left her water jar beside the well and ran back to the village, telling everyone." John 4:28

"The harvesters are paid good wages, and the fruit they harvest is people brought to eternal life. What joy awaits both the planter and the harvester alike." John 4:36

Day 47: Do you really trust Him?

This scripture is clear and to the point. God says in Proverbs 3:5-6, "Trust in the Lord with all your heart; do not depend on your own understanding. Seek his will in all you do, and He will show you which path to take.

Once we choose to desire the will of God for our lives, He will direct your path. He leads us the way we should go. When circumstances and situations look dim, we as believers need to go to God and ask Him what we should do. His promise is that, as long as we place our trust in Him, and not what our eyes see or ears hear, He will show you which path to take.

Just because it looks and sounds great, doesn't mean it was sent by God! Some opportunities, are actually oppositions and some oppositions could be a good opportunity. God will send what is GOOD! He will give discernment. Don't fail the test just because of blindness. You can't see what is behind that door. God can!!!

So you can either choose your path, and go in circles; or His path, and be led into your destiny.

"Trust in the Lord with all your heart, And lean not on your own understanding; In all your ways acknowledge Him, And He shall direct your paths." Proverbs 3:5-6

Day 18: It's a hurting world; We have to pray.

Before, when I heard about the terrible things that were happening in this world and especially in my hometown, it tore my heart. I completely stop watching the news and kept wondering, "why is all this happening?" I just didn't understand.

God is looking for believers to come to him boldly and submit a prayer for our city, our country, this nation. We sit back and talk about who we don't want to become our president, yet the majority of us wouldn't even go out and vote. We have to set aside idle words if we don't have anything good to add to it. If we want great leadership, pray. If we want to change in our city, pray. If we want things to changes in our relationship, pray.

This is the world we live in. Changes can be made if we set in our mind that change needs to be made. If we become complacent to it, it will stay the same. The same devil that is in control of this evil world also has to submit to God!!!! Everything we need was conquered on the cross. As believers, we can't just sit back and not do anything. We can go to God and Pray.

Lord, thank you that I can come boldly to your throne of grace. Make me sensitive to the needs of others, and seek your love through the gift of prayer. Lord, help me not to turn a deaf ear and blind eye to what is going on around me. I pray Lord for all of those who are hurting and feel as if they are alone, those who are struggling and feeling lost, all those who are unemployed and don't know where their next meal will come from. You alone Lord provides everything we need. Our hope and trust is in You. In Jesus name I ask and pray. Amen

Day 49: Today

Today, I will not let past failures haunt me. Even though my life is scarred with mistakes, I refuse to rummage through my trash heap of failures. I will admit them. I will correct them. I will press on. Victoriously! No failure is fatal. It is ok to stumble because you will get back up. Today, I will make a difference. Today, I will listen to my heart. Today, I will discern and heed the voice of the Lord. Today, I will give it my best. Today, I will smile, even if I feel like crying. Today is a blessed day. Today is a day that the Lord has given me. Today, I will not focus on my faults. Today, I will work as if I am working unto the Lord. Today, I will do something different that will elevate me. Today, I will put in the job application or send the resume. Today, I will start my book. Today, I will go to the gym, even though I may feel out of place. Today, I will have peace, joy, happiness, regardless of what the world is showing me. Today is a good day. I will rejoice on TODAY.

I will make my today better than my yesterday.

Day 50: You are already approved

We tend to seek acceptance and recognition from people. We all search for a sense of importance. Social media has wrecked the minds of so many people. It has become a major distraction in the world. We focus on "how many followers we have," "how many likes we have." Our focus can shift from what God has placed in us to what the world sees in us. This boasting can cause arrogance and a sense of pride. If you choose to be "a friend of the word" then by all means, you will allow the world to place you on a fake pedestal.

Once you become a child of the Most High God, the only boasting should be what Jesus Christ did for us all. The elevation that He does, is the elevation that you need. God created you perfect. When He made you, He was pleased. Yes, we all will go through periods in our lives where we have to be broken and rebuilt, yet God has already made you a masterpiece. You are His workmanship. You are already approved to do His good works.

It doesn't matter how many friends you have (that you may NEVER really know), how many likes or followers you have; not a single one of them died for your sins. Let the world see the Light inside of you instead of having the light placed on you. No one is that important.

Blessings

"For we are His workmanship, created in Christ Jesus for good works, which God prepared beforehand that we should walk in them." Ephesians 2:10

Day 51: Confusion During Times of Loss

Have you ever been blindsided by a personal disaster? Sometimes trouble brews slowly, and you can see it coming. But other times the blow falls without any warning. You are given a cancer diagnosis...a tragic car accident leaves you or a loved one disabled.

The loss is bad enough. What makes it worse is the fog of confusion. A sudden loss can really disrupt your peace of mind. Why didn't God stop this from happening?

God is not only in control of the universe in general, but he is closely monitoring your life in particular. He takes inventory of every hair on your head. He further promises to make absolutely every one of your life experiences — the joyful ones and the miserable ones — work for you.

He is an unshakeable rock you can stand on, written by a man who experienced plenty of hardships: "We know that in all things God works for the good of those who love him, who have been called according to his purposes" (Romans 8:28). Did you get that? At this very moment, God is working for your good in whatever situation you faced or has ever struggled with. It may still hurt just dealing with the situation, but know on today, that your Heavenly Father is walking out your every step. Glory to God.

Day 52: It's Time To Sing a New Song

There are times when talking, crying and stressing about it is over. It is now time to start rejoicing for what God is doing. It will come a time that you will have to turn the page to a new chapter. Stop singing the same old sad tune that you have sung so long, and "Sing a new song unto the Lord." Psalms 96:1

God who is the Creator of Heaven and Earth knew you and had already ordained your every step. He has placed victory of a new song in you. A delay doesn't mean a denial. Your request has been answered! God could be working in you to prepare you for what He has already done.

Acknowledge your failures, addictions, hardships, struggles, pain, and trials. Lay them at His feet. Don't hold on to things that hurt you. Why worry when the Word says, "Don't worry about anything; instead, pray about everything. Tell God what you need, and thank him for all He has done." Jesus said in Mark 11:24, "When you pray, believe that you have received it, and you will have it."

The only reason we continue to pray about "old songs," is because we remember our fear in our failures. And we are not "sure" if it will happen. We feel like we know ourselves and our "major issues" better than God does. But when we place complete trust and total reliance only in God, He will work it out. He not only cares about the big problems, but He also cares about the smallest ones.

Day 53: Preparation to Elevate

The things in your past did not happen to define you, it happened to prepare you. Not everyone will see and understand the dreams and visions God has placed in you. Regardless of what the world has thrown at you, continue to speak the Word of God over your marriage, children, health, finances, career, business or anything else that is connected to you. There is life and death in the power of your tongue. If you only speak what you see, then what you see will confuse you all the time. Whatever situation you are dealing with today, go to the Word of God and find scripture that pertains to it. If it anger, find something on anger. If you are having a hard time in your finances, then find scriptures on wealth and prosperity. If you are struggling in your marriage, find scriptures on marriage. If your children are rebelling, find scriptures regarding the promises of God over your descendants. Every situation or problem we deal with in everyday life, is in the Bible.

Even if your situation hasn't changed when you have prayed about it, trust that God has already heard and has answered. Be patient, speak life and watch what He will do right in front of your eyes.

So be thankful for your struggles, hardships, and pains. You will see later, that they were points of elevation.

"But as for you, you meant evil against me; but God meant it for good, in order to bring it about as it is this day, to save many people alive." Genesis 50:20

"Death and life are in the power of the tongue, and those who love it will eat its fruit." Proverbs 18:22

"Dear brothers and sisters, when troubles of any kind come your way, consider it an opportunity for great joy," James 1:2

Day 54: Words full of Seed

The words that we speak can be some of the most powerful things we have to deal with. They can either build someone up or tear them down. In the midst of an argument or disagreement, we all tend to say things that we very seldom regret. We all want to get the last word or just yell louder than the other person to get our point across. When all of this is happening, I can just imagine the devil standing in the corner just laughing and having a ball at what he has initiated. Wouldn't you hate knowing that you could possibly be giving power to the enemy?

Once we put on the whole Armor of God, we can stand firm knowing that He will fight our battles. It's never worth losing your temper over a petty disagreement or getting sick after an argument that could have been prevented.

Even when you have left this world, your words will still remain. What words or seeds are you planting in others? Are you lifting people up or tearing them down with what you speak over them? Always remember, your words are not just powerful for you, they are powerful for others too.

"Put on God's armor so that you will be able to stand firm against all strategies of the devil." Ephesian 6:11

Day 55: Your Dream

God has placed dreams and vision within us all. The more you tap into His Word, the more He will give you a glimpse of what His plan is for you. Most of the time when God has given you a dream, and you speak it, most people are not going to believe it. Joseph's brothers not only hated him for telling them the dream, but they also hated him for "speaking" it. "His brothers responded, "So you think you will be our king, do you? Do you actually think you will reign over us? And they hated him all the more because of his dreams and the way he talked about them." Genesis 37:8

Joseph was excited. He had joy in knowing that God had shown him this dream.

Most of the time, it may be the ones closest to you who will not believe your vision. You tell them what your future plans are, your dreams and your goals. They respond with, "Yeah, that's great." Yet they do not believe a word you are saying. They don't believe because they know the person you use to be. They know your failures, background, struggles and past mistakes. How would God be able to use you? You have too much behind you for God to actually use you. Smile and continue to trust what God has shown you.

Your past may indeed cause you to have limited opportunities; yet we serve a limitless God. When you let go of striving, and just rest; God will work on your behalf. God bless

Day 56: Timing is Everything

Timing is everything. A lot of things in our lives are surrounded by TIME. Ecclesiastes 3 teaches us that there is a time for everything. As believers, we have to listen to the voice of the Holy Spirit to know when the time is right. When we rush to get things finished, we may make a mess of it and have to start over. But when you are "still in the presence of the Lord and wait on Him to act," Psalms 37:1, 1 Peter 5:6 says that He will "Exalt you in due time."

We all have choices to make. We could allow man to use their so-called power to exalt you or wait and let God exalt you. Man will probably get you there faster; but you will fall just as fast. With God, the way UP is by humbling yourself and trusting His direction. God is more concerned about your permanent growth than your temporary gain.

"Rest in the Lord, and wait patiently for Him; Do not fret because of him who prospers in his way, Because of the man who brings wicked schemes to pass." Psalms 37:7

Day 57: Forgiving in advance

Prior to Jesus sitting with the disciples at the last supper, He had just spoken to them all and said, "One of you sitting here with me will betray Me." Jesus had already known in advance that Judas was going to betray Him.

As I sit here and study this scripture, it takes me back to a time when I had so much unforgiveness in my heart. I was stressed, hurting all the time, angry, high blood pressure, depressed and working sometimes 14 days in a row to drown my pain. Staying busy hid my true emotions. I was so ashamed that I didn't want to even go back to the place where the problem existed. I didn't want to go home. I allowed that one event to define my destiny. As I stood in that shower in 2012, all I could hear from God was "forgive you." I didn't realize that my hurt and pain was stemming from my own unforgiveness of me.

As Jesus and the disciples sat there at the table and after He had just told them, "one of you will betray Me," He still shared His bread with them. He didn't leave Judas out; He included them all. He had already forgiven Judas in advance.

Most of us will go each and every day with bitterness and unforgiveness in our hearts for so many years. We continue to focus on our past instead of living in the present and hopeful for the future. We tend to take up residence in it. Judas couldn't even forgive himself, so his own shame and regret, caused his own untimely death. We don't need someone approval to be happy, but we do need to let go of past hurt and pain that was either caused by someone else or even your own failures. Forgive, let it go and trust that God will work it out for your good.

Day 58: Passion or Purpose

As I come to a close on this journey, I am brought to passion vs purpose. That has to be a question you have more than likely asked of God. "Lord, what is my purpose?" Most of the time, our Heavenly Father shows us our purpose every single day, but because we do not tangibly see it, we miss it. We can miss it by getting too comfortable in where we are, listening to other voices or just too afraid to walk into it. This brings me to the story of the man at the pool of Bethesda. He had been lying there for 38 years waiting for someone to come and help him get in the pool. When Jesus asked him, "Do you want to be made well?" He answered Him with an excuse. How many times has someone asked you what your plans are for your life, and your first answer was an excuse? Could your excuse be the reason why you haven't walked in your purpose? Could it be the reason you still live in lack? Could it be the reason you haven't excelled in school? Could it be the reason you haven't lost weight? Could it be the reason you haven't moved to a new level of the destiny God had already given you? Today, do not allow your passion to block your purpose. Your passion is what you chose to do; your purpose is what God called you do. Seek first the kingdom of God, and He will speak to you.

"When Jesus saw him lying there, and knew that he already had been in that condition a long time, He said to him, "Do you want to be made well?" John 5:6

"But seek first the kingdom of God and His righteousness, and all these things shall be added to you." Matthew 6:33 NKJV

Day 59: Even NOW

Today…today, you will be faced with multiple tests, trials, more than likely many distractions. You will probably question God about why is all this happening to you. You will probably cry tears of pain or joy. You will sit and wonder "what next Lord"? Well, I am in that same place with you. God desires to get us from our Now to our Next. Life is a journey. And we are all on our own road to our destiny. It may get tough, it may be hard, it may seem as if you are ready to give up, yet God is again breaking you down to build you back up.

As I sit here and think on Jesus and His suffering on the road to Golgotha, it reminds me that we all have to go through in order to get to the Promise Land. When the Israelites were led through the Red Sea on ground, they had to go through. In our natural sight, there is no way possible that they would have gotten to the other side if God had not made a way. Even NOW, Jesus is your Way, even NOW He has a plan for you, even NOW blessings are waiting on you, even NOW He wants to rain favor on you, even NOW your problems are not bigger than His promise, even NOW in this day, all your sins have been washed away. God desires a relationship with you "JUST AS YOU ARE!" There is nothing you or I can do to become better for HIM. We have to trust that God knows best for us. Yes, there is better. Today may have started off as a tough day for you, but even NOW, He is with you. So, don't give up or give in. When it seems to get hard, know that the SON is in the midst of all the storms. Even though He didn't cause them, He will cause all things to work together for your good. EVEN ON TODAY. Blessings

"Do you now believe." John 16:31

"And now these three things remain: faith, hope, and love. But the greatest of these is love." 1 Corinthians 13:13

Day 60: Living your prayers

As I sit and write the last devotion, I am led to write about what God said to me when I was restored. When I was going through my wilderness, I knew God would give me back all that I had lost, yet it is all that I saw. I prayed about it day and night, I journaled about it, I cried about it, it was all that I thought about. I remember writing down the exact place we desired to live, the job I wanted; down to the hospital, the pay I wanted and the drive in minutes. That was all I could see. Was me. It was all about me.

So as I was driving to my apt in the city I desired, I remember the Holy Spirit saying to me "you are living your prayers." I felt like it was so loud. It took me to another place. I literally had chill rushing through my body as I was driving. It was an "aha moment." At that moment, I knew that I could change my prayers. I didn't have to just accept what I was seeing. I could go to God in prayer, and if my prayers lined up with His will, it would be done for me. The same goes for you. God desires to give you more than your eyes can see. He wants to show you how much He loves you. If you could have anything in the world, what would it be? Does it line up with the Word of God?

So, whatever prayers, dreams, visions or goals you have desired, can happen. God has literally given us the power to speak life into our situation. He has given us the power to speak those things that are not as though they were. He has created power in us to create. To create our life, to create our vision and to create our goals.

Today, you have the choice to create all you desire. As long as it is in alignment with the will of God; with patience, perseverance, and most importantly PRAYER, it will come to fruition.

༻ Devotional Notes ༺   Date:

❦ Devotional Notes ❦ Date:

❧ Devotional Notes ❧   Date:

~ Devotional Notes ~ Date:

❦ Devotional Notes ❦   Date:

∞ Devotional Notes ∞   Date:

❧ Devotional Notes ❧   Date:

❧ Devotional Notes ❧   Date:

❧ Devotional Notes ❧   Date:

❧ Devotional Notes ☙   Date:

Devotional Notes   Date:

www.ingramcontent.com/pod-product-compliance
Lightning Source LLC
Chambersburg PA
CBHW061443040426
42450CB00007B/1181